# Stitching with Hugs 'n Kisses

## Favourite Embroidery Stitches

HELEN STUBBINGS

Publisher, Editor, Illustrator, Photographer: Helen Stubbings
Distribution enquiries:
Pattern Press PO Box 390 Lenah Valley TAS Australia 7008
Phone:+61 3 62787507
Email: *orders@patternpress.com.au*
Website: *www.patternpress.com.au*

National Library of Australia Cataloguing-in-Publication entry

Author: Stubbings, Helen, 1967-
Title: Stitching with Hugs 'n Kisses : favourite embroidery stitches / written, illustrated and photographed by Helen Stubbings.
ISBN: 9780975744420 (pbk.)
Subjects: Embroidery.
Fancy work.
Dewey Number: 746.44

Printed in China Through Red Planet Print Management

A simple stitch book for easy reference. 12 basic, useable and very do-able stitches to grow your skills inventory.
Use them in your stitchery and embroidery projects, download my free practice projects and then perfect them as you stitch my patterns. I hope I continue to inspire, share, grow and teach you exciting and feelgood things so that you too may enjoy my passion of stitching.

hugs......Helen

# Contents:

Needles:
A Crewel needle is required to get good results when working most of the stitches in this book. I use a #7 Crewel or Hugs'n Kisses Stitchery needle for almost all of my work.
This size needle suits the size of my designs and the size of thread I mainly use. The needle size is dependant on the thickness of thread you are using.
A Straw or Milliner needle is useful for stitching Bullion knots.

Embroidery Hoop:
I ALWAYS use an embroidery hoop to work my stitches. Rather than to keep the fabric tight I use it as an extra hand. There are two methods of stitching - Stab stitching and Scoop stitching. I use a scoop method as shown in the diagrams in this book. For scoop stitching have the fabric slightly loose in the hoop and use your finger underneath the hoop to assist in bringing the needle back to the front with each stitch. An embroidery hoop assists in gaining good tension and even perfect stitches.

Threads:
My threads of choice are Presencia Finca Perle #16 threads - equivalent to 1½ strands of a stranded cotton they are a perfect size to cover my design lines, reel off a roll without having to split strands and have a lovely perle sheen. Almost any thread of choice can be used when making these embroidery stitches - play and experiment.

Stabiliser:
I always apply a stabiliser to the back of my embroidery work before stitching. The type of stabiliser chosen is dependant on the final use of the piece. I may use a very lightweight fusible batting or a lightweight fusible woven interfacing type product. The stabiliser keeps your work and tension neat, allows beginning and ending with knots and allows small thread travels across the back of your work...... yes these are things not allowed by the embroidery police but for me, it's all about having fun, enjoying the process, achieving a quick and self satisfying result and no-one is going to see the back anyway :)

# Running Stitch

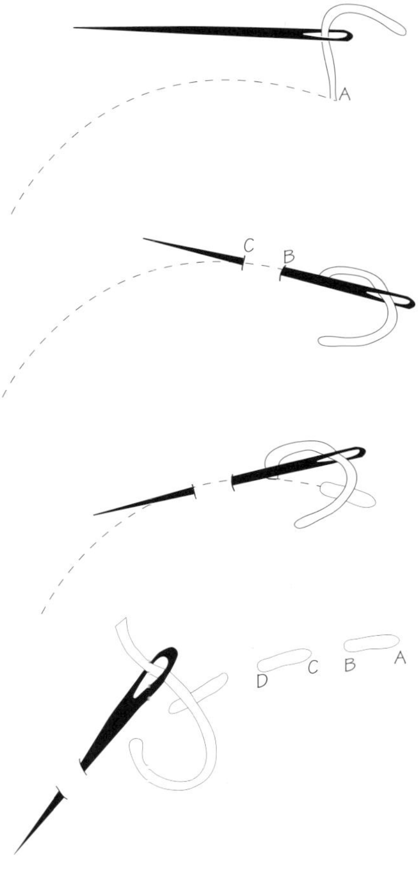


Running stitch is the simplest and most basic of all stitches which can be used to build up patterns and texture.

It can be worked in many threads and even ribbons.

It is used as a quilting stitch. It can be used as a light outline stitch.

It is generally worked from right to left but is achievable in any direction.

<u>For perfect stitches:</u>

*If following a line use a sharp pointed needle and pierce the centre of the marked line with every stitch.

*Keep the top stitches an even length and the spaces an even length.

*The stitch length and the space length do not have to be the same.

# Back Stitch

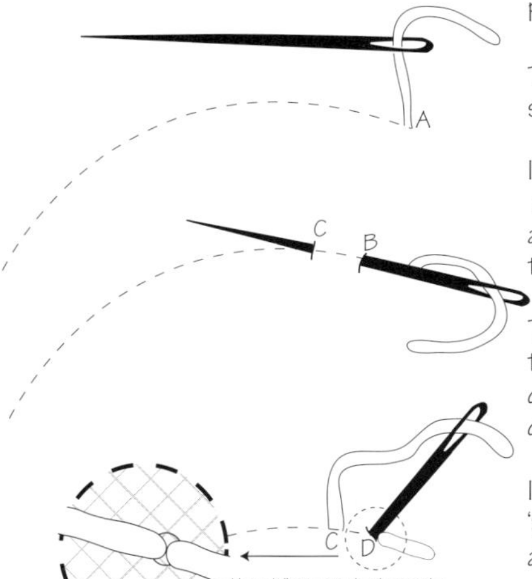


Note: When going back into the previous stitch you must go into the exact same hole for a perfect stitch. That is points B and D are the same.

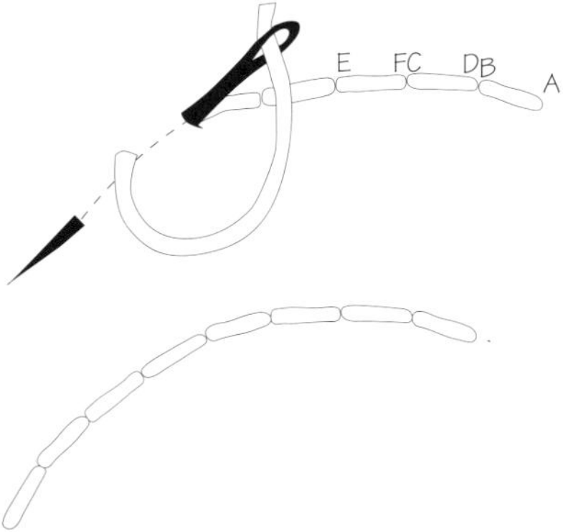


Back Stitch is also known as Point de Sable.

The Back Stitch is a great outline stitch used to cover line work.

It can follow intricate curves well if the stitches are worked in small even lengths to follow the flow of the curve.

They can be worked in almost any thread with the size dependant on the size of your design.

It is commonly used in simple 'Stitchery' designs to cover all the lines of a pictorial design.

The stitch can be worked from right to left or towards or away from yourself - turn your hoop as you work around curves.

On the back of your work it will appear as a Stem Stitch.

<u>For perfect stitches:</u>

*Each stitch should go into the exact same hole as the previous stitch.

*Use a sharp needle to pierce the marked line in the exact centre to get nice straight lines.

*Keep the stitch lengths even.

# Stem Stitch

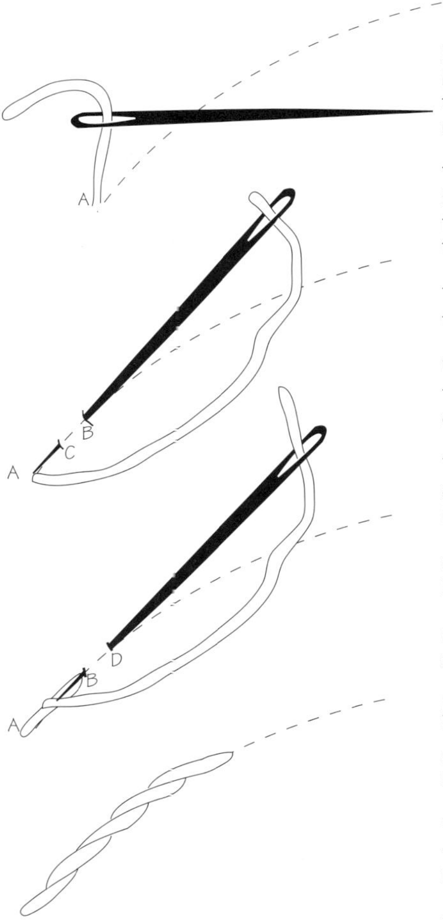


The Stem Stitch is another great outline stitch to cover line work.

It will give a slightly heavier look than the Backstitch. It is the traditional stitch used for redwork embroidery.

The Outline Stitch is a variation - it is the same except that the thread is kept above the needle instead of below.

The stitch is worked from left to right.

When choosing Stem or Outline try to keep the thread to the outside of a curve.

Tight curves may need an occasional couching stitch to keep stitches in place.

On curved lines keep the stitch length small and even.

On the back of your work it will appear as a Backstitch.

<u>For perfect stitches:</u>
*Every time the needle goes in or out of the fabric it should be in the centre of the line.

*Each stitch should overlap the previous stitch by half of its length.

*Keep the stitch lengths even.

# Chain Stitch

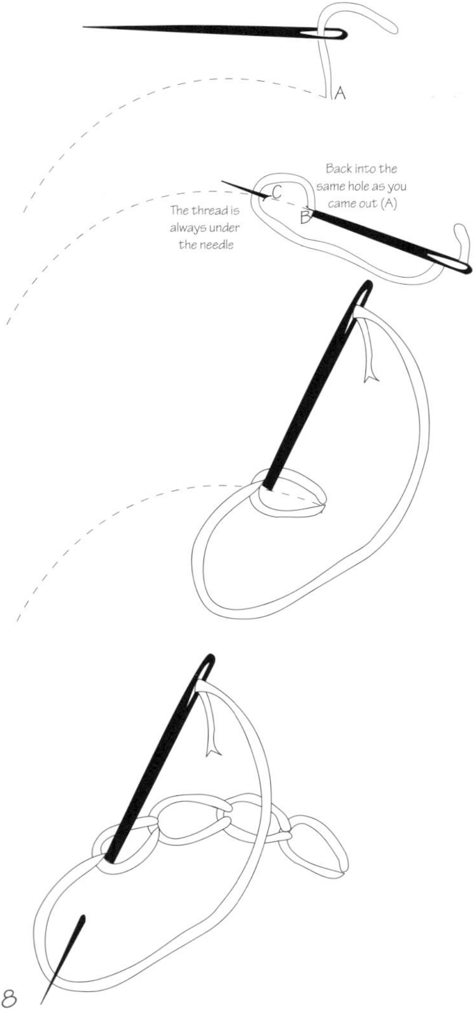


Chain Stitch is also known as Tambour Stitch and Point de Chainette.

Chain Stitch is one of the oldest of the decorative stitches and has many variations.

It can be worked in many threads and even ribbons.

It can be used as an outline stitch for line work and will give a heavier line than both Back and Stem Stitch.

It is generally worked from right to left or away from you.

It can also be used as a filler stitch.

For Perfect stitches:

*Points A and B are the same hole or thereabouts.

*The needle should enter and exit always on the marked line.

*Keep the stitch lengths even.

*For a solid line use smaller stitches.

*Do not pull the thread too tight when laying under the needle.

# Detached Chain or Lazy Daisy

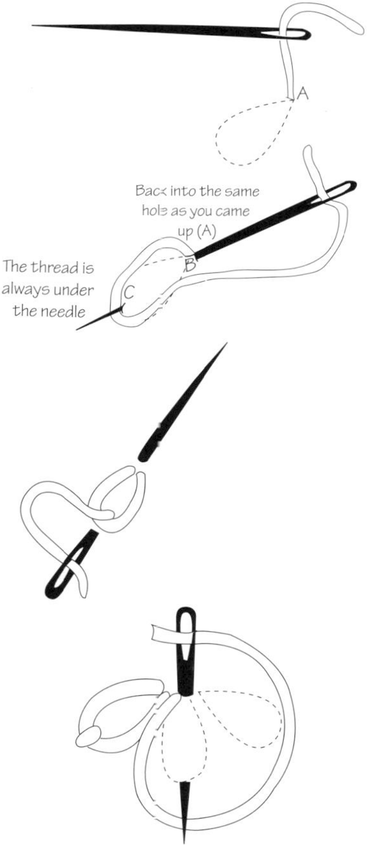


This stitch is often worked in a circle to form a flower motif and as a result is also known as Lazy Daisy Stitch.

It can be worked in many thread types and even ribbons.

It can be used for flowers and leaves as a group or singly.

It can be worked as a double or triple detached chain (one inside the other) for more solid shapes.

For perfect stitches:

*Points A and B are the same hole or thereabouts.

*Keep the stitch lengths even.

*Do not pull the thread too tight when laying under the needle. You want a nice curve on your petal or leaf.

*It is best to keep this stitch fairly short - maximum of approx 6mm/¼" to achieve nice curved petals which stay in

# Buttonhole or Blanket Stitch

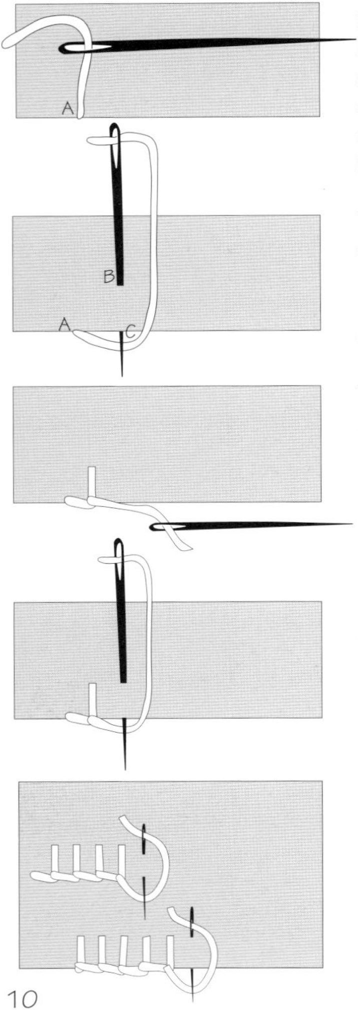


Blanket Stitch is named because it was often used as an edging on blankets. It is also commonly known as Buttonhole Stitch (although a traditional Buttonhole Stitch is slightly different).

This stitch is worked from left to right over two imaginary lines.

It can be worked along a straight edge or around curves.

Tight curves may need an occasional couching stitch to keep stitches in place.

It can be varied by changing the length of each portion of the stitch, stitching on angles or even up and down.

<u>For perfect stitches:</u>

*For a traditional even Blanket Stitch keep each element of the stitch (the top and both sides) the same length.

*When stitching around curves or a corner take the thread through to the back and then back up inside to couch the stitch into position.

*Do not over tighten the stitch and pucker the fabric.

# Satin Stitch

Satin Stitch is also known as Damask Stitch.

As one of the oldest embroidery stitches to be found it is worked by embroiderer's on traditional designs in practically every country.

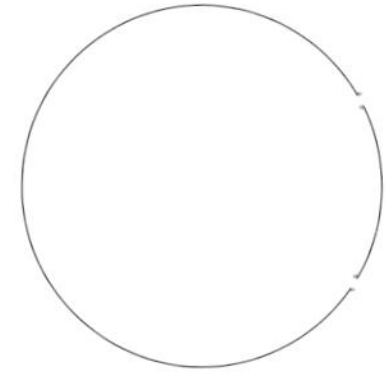

Backstitch or Split stitch outline first

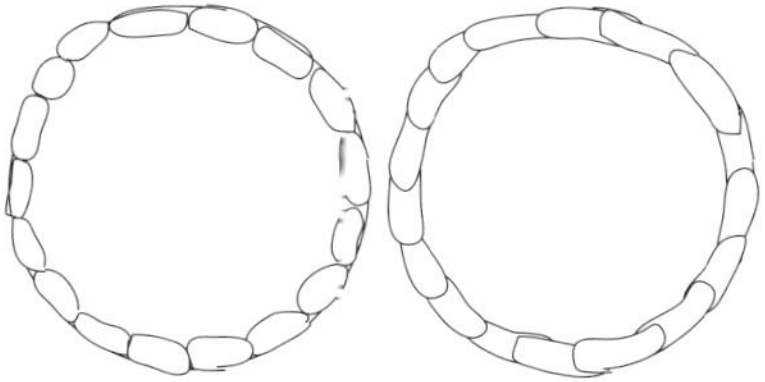

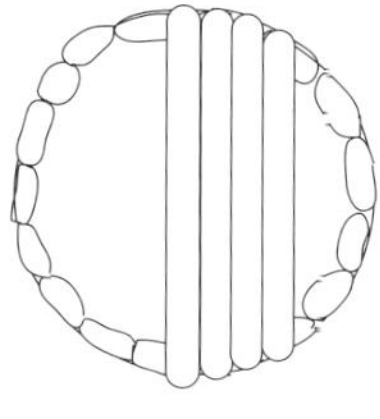

Satin stitch over the top

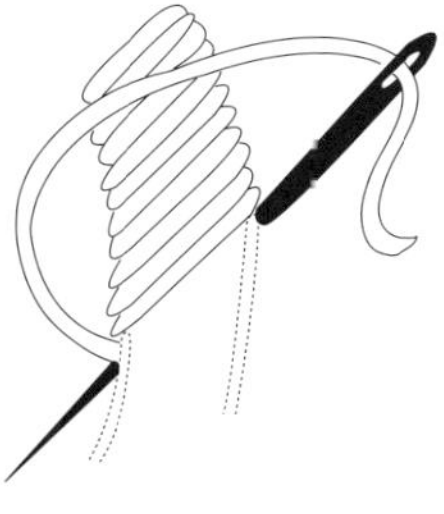

<u>For perfect stitches:</u>

*Outline your shape first using a back or split stitch.

*Keep all stitches horizontal or vertical and lay them carefully side by side.

*Do not let the stitches sit on top of each other, they must sit side by side.

*For a circle I like to start in the centre and stitch to one side, then the other.

*Do not pull the thread too tight and distort the fabric.

*Keep your thread untwisted for a nice smooth sheen to your stitch.

# French Knot

The French Knot is the best known and used knot stitch.

It is used for dots or as a filler stitch.

The size of the knot is determined by the size of the thread used.

A true knot has only one wrap, you may be able to do 2-3 wraps and successfully get a larger knot.

For a Pistil Stitch take the needle back down into the fabric away from point A where you came up.

French Knots can tend to be lazy and lay down - if you need precise positioning use a Colonial Knot.

<u>For perfect stitches:</u>
*A Straw or Milliner needle may assist.

*Always pull the wraps firmly onto the fabric and hold thread taut before taking the needle to the back and pulling the thread through the wraps - if they are left loose you will get loops and messy knots up the thread.

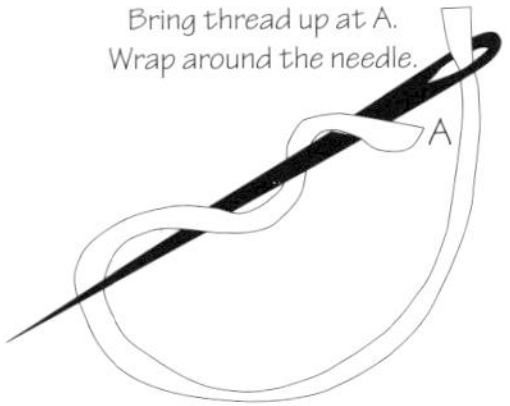


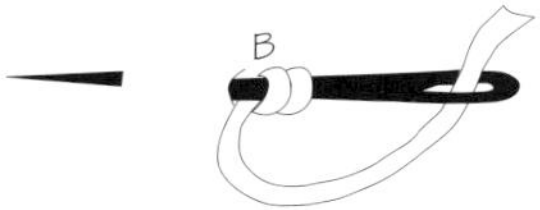


Take the needle back into the fabric one thread away from point A where you came up (not the same hole)
Slide wraps evenly down the needle so that they sit on the fabric.
Take needle to the back of the fabric or into your next position.

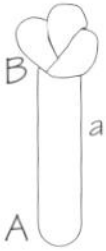


A Pistil Stitch - a straight stitch with a french knot on the end.

# Colonial Knot

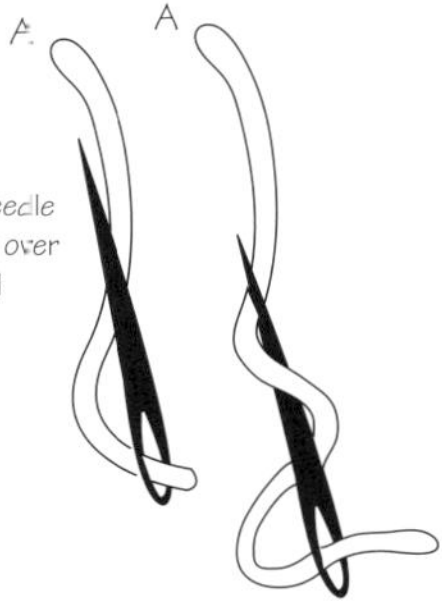


Bring up at A, take the needle to the left under and back over the top of the thread

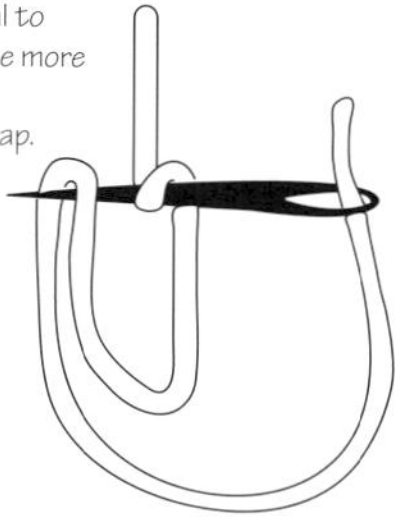

Turn the needle horizontal to you and wrap the thread once more around the needle forming a figure eight wrap.

Pull the knot tight onto the fabric and take the needle down close to point A to finish.

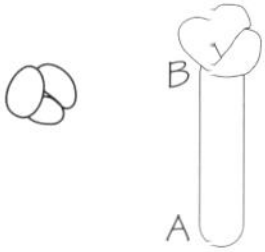


A Pistil Stitch - a straight stitch with a Colonial knot on the end.

The Colonial Knot is also known as a Candlewicking Knot or Figure Eight Knot.

It is used for dots or as a filler stitch.

The size of the knot is determined by the size of the thread used.

A true knot has only one wrap, you may be able to do 2-3 wraps and successfully get a larger knot.

For a Pistil Stitch take the needle back down into the fabric away from point A where you came up.

Candlewicking designs are based on evenly spaced knots to make the design. The Candlewicking or Colonial Knot will sit exactly where it is placed and is best used when exact placement is needed.

For perfect stitches:

*A Straw or Milliner needle may assist.

*Always pull the wraps firmly onto the fabric and hold thread taut before taking the needle to the back and pulling the thread through the wraps - if they are left loose you will get loops and messy knots up the thread.

# Fly Stitch

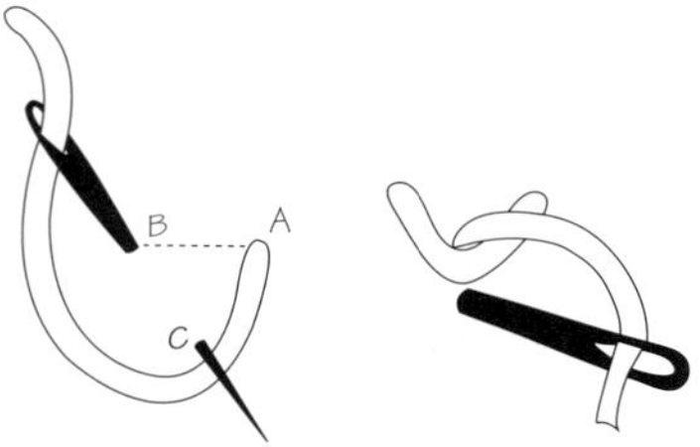


Fly Stitch is also known as 'Y' Stitch or Open Loop Stitch.

It can be worked as a single stitch or a line of stitches.

The stitch can be varied by the length of the vertical straight stitch giving a 'V' or 'Y' appearance.

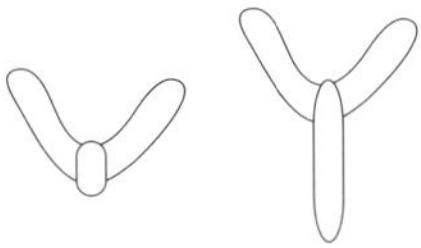

They can be worked in any thread size, wool or ribbon.

I usually work a line of Fly Stitch towards me or from right to left.

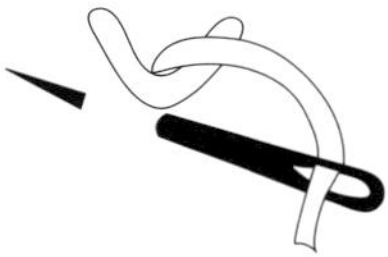

Fly Stitch is used often in Crazy Quilt embroidery.

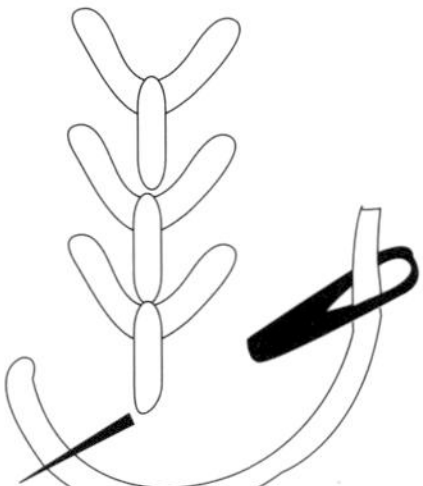

For perfect stitches:

*Keep the A & B points horizontal.

*For an even symmetrical stitch keep the length between A, B & C the same.

# Feather Stitch

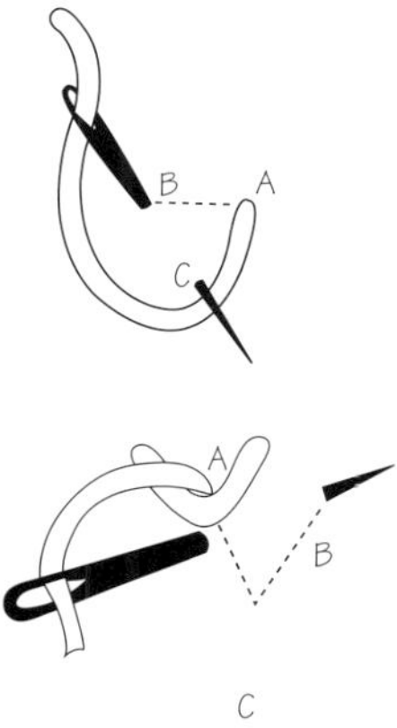


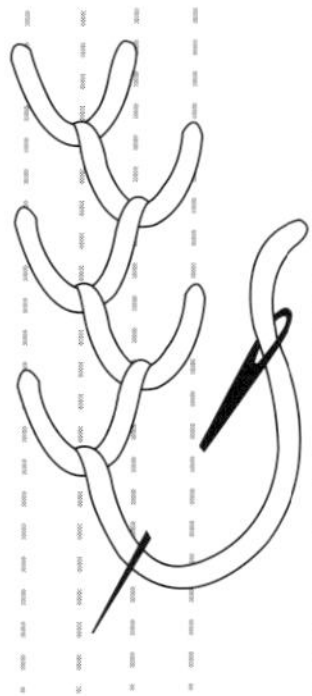

Feather Stitch is also known as Single Coral Stitch and Briar Stitch.

It can be worked on a straight line or a curve.

It is a variation on a Buttonhole or Blanket Stitch.

It can be worked as a single, double or triple Feather Stitch.

It can be worked in any thread size, wool or ribbon.

I usually work a line of Feather Stitch towards me or from right to left.

Drawing up a four line grid may assist when learning this stitch.

Feather stitch is commonly used in Crazy Quilt embroidery. It is also a Smocking Stitch. It can be used in combination with many other stitches.

Double Feather - take two stitches to the right then two to the left

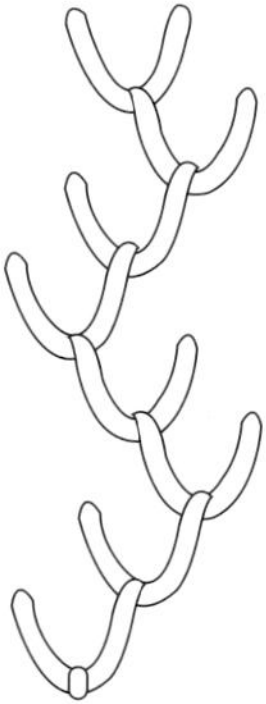

Triple Feather - take three stitches to the right then three to the left

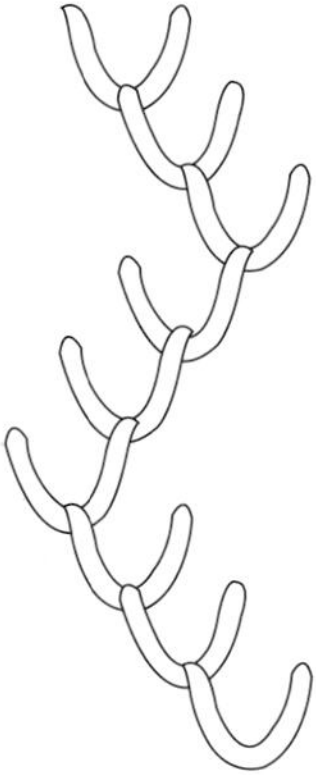

For perfect stitches:

*Keep the A & B points horizontal.

*For an even symmetrical stitch keep the length between A, B & C the same.

# Bullion Knot

Bullion Knot is also known as Bullion Stitch, Caterpillar Stitch, Coil Stitch, Grub Knot, Knot Stitch, Post Stitch, Porto Rico Rose and Worm Stitch.

They can be worked in almost any thread with the size of the thread determining the size of the knot.

They can be straight or curved and used in conjunction with other stitches.

A hoop is recommended so that you have two hands free to make a good knot.

For a straight Bullion wrap enough times to fill the space between A & B. For a curved Bullion wrap more times than is required to fill this space forcing the knotted stitch to curve outwards.

Bullions can be used to make many designs in variations - roses, leaves, animals etc.

<u>For perfect stitches:</u>

*Use a Straw or Milliner needle.

*Use an embroidery hoop.

*Pull the wraps firmly and evenly to the bottom of the needle before pulling thread through to the back.

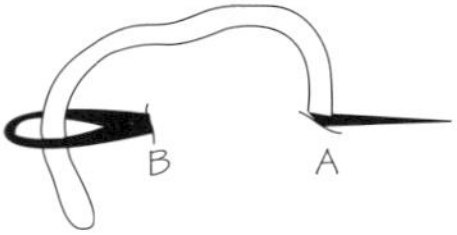

Bring needle up at A , down at B and back up at A leaving a loop.

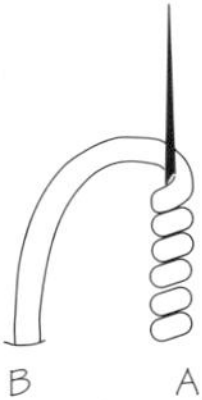

Wrap the thread around the needle enough times to cover the distance between A and B

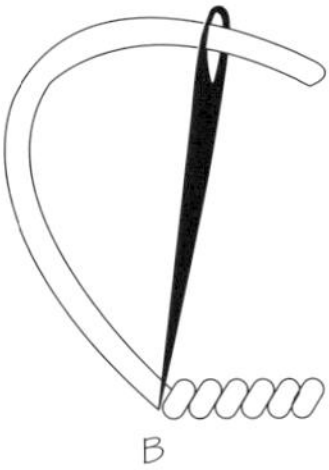

Hold the wraps tightly on the needle as you pull the thread through the loops. Take the needle down at B to anchor your wrapped Bullion Stitch.

# Herringbone Stitch

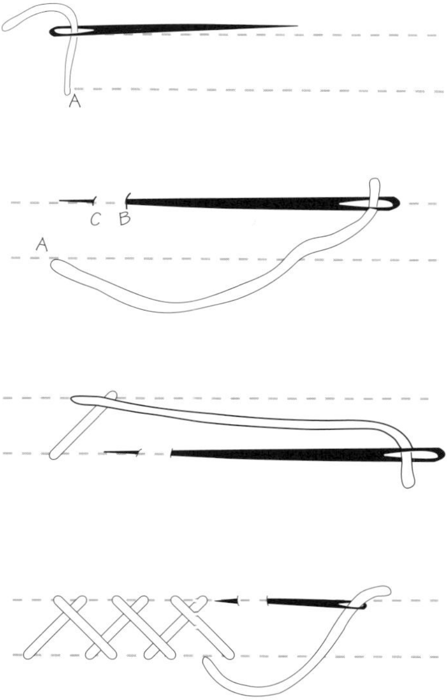


Herringbone Stitch is also known as Mossoul Stitch, Russian Stitch, Plaited Stitch, Catch Stitch and Witch Stitch.

It can be worked in almost any thread or ribbon.

The stitch is generally worked from left to right.

Two marked or imaginary parallel lines will assist when learning.

The spacing of your stitches can give many appearances to this stitch.

It is commonly used in Crazy Quilt Embroidery and can be combined with other stitches.

For perfect stitches:
*Every entry and exit of the needle should be on the marked or imaginary line.

*For a traditional symmetrical stitch keep the stitch length and spacing even.

# Chevron Stitch

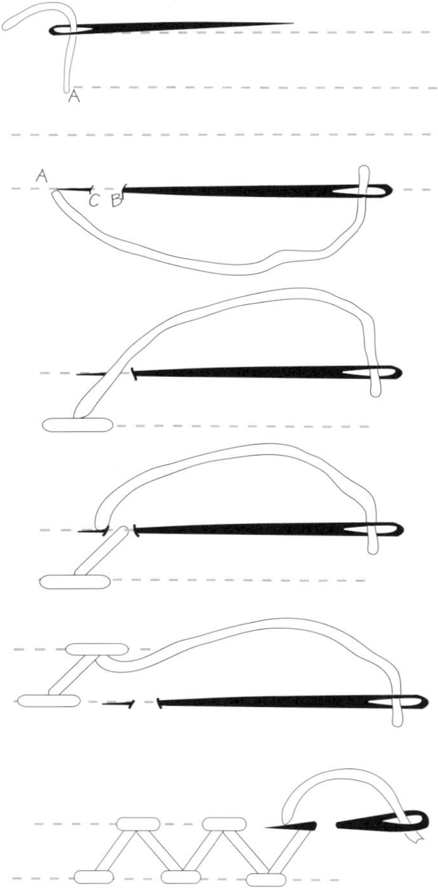


Chevron Stitch is a variety of Herringbone Stitch and worked with a similar way.

Chevron Stitch is generally worked from left to right on two parallel lines.

Whilst normally stitched on straight lines it can be worked around gentle curves by adjusting the inner curve stitch length.

It is widely used in Crazy Quilt embroidery and can be combined with many other stitches.

Marking temporary parallel lines may assist when learning for an even stitch.

Different effects can be achieved by altering the angle and spacing of your stitches.

For Perfect stitches:

*Each entry and exit point of the needle should be on a marked or imaginary line.

*For a traditional symmetrical stitch keep the length of each segment even.

If you need more assistance in learning these stitches
please visit my 'Stitched Sunday' blog pages

http://hugsnkisses.typepad.com/hugsfromhelen/stitchedsunday/

where you will find step by step photo tutorials on each stitch.
At the bottom of each stitch lesson you will also find a link to download and print a ***free pattern*** design to practice and perfect your new stitch!
There is even a free pattern to make your very own stitch book to showcase your work.

Please stitch, enjoy and share your accomplishments. Can I just ask if you do share these free patterns to please include the original link to the downloads rather than copying and sharing.

Please also download my free 'Hugs 'n Kisses' App. This App has direct links to all of the stitch diagrams and tutorials so you can carry them with you wherever you may be stitching.
Available in the I-Tunes store.

Enjoy the passion of stitching!

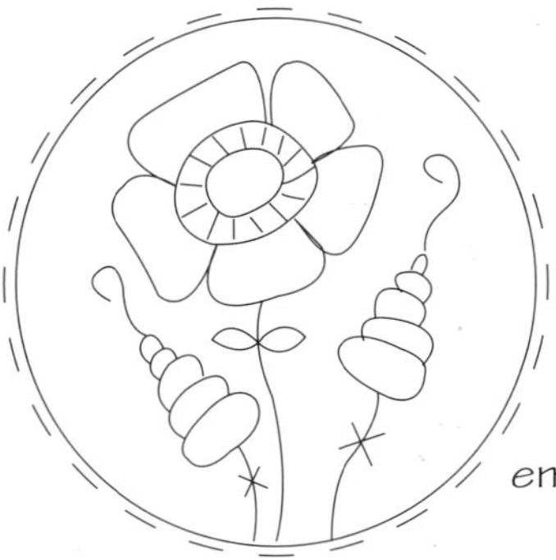

email: helen@hugsnkisses.net
web:www.hugsnkisses.net
blog: www.hugsnkisses.typepad.com
facebook: www.facebook.com/helenshugsnkisses